Copyright © 2023 by Adriana Shannon (Author)

This book is protected by copyright law and is intended solely for personal use. Reproduction, distribution, or any other form of use requires the written permission of the author. The information presented in this book is for educational and entertainment purposes only, and while every effort has been made to ensure its accuracy and completeness, no guarantees are made. The author is not providing legal, financial, medical, or professional advice, and readers should consult with a licensed professional before implementing any of the techniques discussed in this book. The content in this book has been sourced from various reliable sources, but readers should exercise their own judgment when using this information. The author is not responsible for any losses, direct or indirect, that may occur from the use of this book, including but not limited to errors, omissions, or inaccuracies.

We hope this book has been informative and helpful on your journey to understanding and celebrating older adults. Thank you for your interest and support!

Title: Trials of the Heart: Finding Love and Purpose
Subtitle: Overcoming Obstacles to Discover Your True Calling

Series: Legends Unfulfilled: The Story of Football's Greatest Talents Forced to Retire Early
By Adriana Shannon

"Football is a universal language that brings people together from all over the world, regardless of their differences."
Pele, former Brazilian international footballer

"Some people believe football is a matter of life and death, I am very disappointed with that attitude. I can assure you it is much, much more important than that."
Bill Shankly, former Liverpool FC manager

"Football is a simple game. Twenty-two men chase a ball for 90 minutes and at the end, the Germans always win."
Gary Lineker, former England international footballer

"I once cried because I had no shoes to play football, but one day, I met a man who had no feet."
Zinedine Zidane, former French international footballer and coach

"Football is a game of mistakes. Whoever makes the fewest mistakes wins."
Johan Cruyff, former Dutch international footballer and coach

"Football is the most important of the least important things in life."
Carlo Ancelotti, Italian football coach

"Football is not just about scoring goals, it's about creating moments of magic that will live forever in the memory of the fans."
Ronaldinho, former Brazilian international footballer

Table of Contents

Introduction 7
Introducing the players of this Book 7
The challenges and triumphs of professional football 10
Setting the stage for the stories of these players 13

Chapter 1: Ronaldo (31, retired in 2011) 15
The early years of Ronaldo's career 15
Rise to fame and success with Manchester United 18
The move to Real Madrid and continued success 20
The later years and retirement from professional football 22

Chapter 2: Kieron Dyer (32, retired in 2013) 24
The beginnings of Dyer's career with Ipswich Town 24
The move to Newcastle United and rise to prominence .. 27
Injuries and setbacks in later career 29
Retirement and life after football 31

Chapter 3: David Busst (30, retired in 1996) 33
The early years and rise to professional football 33
The infamous injury that ended his career 36
Coping with the aftermath and life after football 39
Reflections on the impact of the injury 42

Chapter 4: Djibril Cisse (34, retired in 2015) 45
The early years and rise to prominence with Auxerre ... 45
Success with Liverpool and the France national team ... 47

5

Injuries and setbacks in later career *50*

Retirement and life after football *52*

Chapter 5: Gueida Fofana (25, retired in 2018) **55**

The early years and rise to professional football *55*

Success with Lyon and the France youth teams *59*

The injury that forced early retirement *62*

Coping with the aftermath and life after football *64*

Chapter 6: Dean Ashton (26, retired in 2009) **66**

The early years and rise to prominence with Crewe Alexandra *66*

The move to Norwich City and continued success *68*

Injuries and setbacks in later career *71*

Retirement and life after football *73*

Conclusion **75**

Reflections on the stories of these players *75*

The challenges and rewards of a career in professional football *78*

Looking ahead to the future of the sport and its players *80*

Key Terms and Definitions **83**

Supporting Materials **85**

Introduction
Introducing the players of this Book

Football is a sport that has captivated millions of people around the world. The passion, the energy, and the excitement that surrounds it are unparalleled. And while we often marvel at the talent of the best players on the pitch, we sometimes forget the challenges and struggles they face, both on and off the field.

This book series is dedicated to some of the most talented players in football history who had to retire too early due to serious injury. These players were at the top of their game, but their careers were cut short, leaving us to wonder what might have been.

In this book series, we will explore the stories of six players who embodied the heart and soul of the game. From the highs of success to the lows of injury and retirement, we will follow their journeys and gain a deeper understanding of what it takes to make it as a professional footballer.

Chapter 1 focuses on Ronaldo, one of the greatest players of his generation. We will explore his early years and rise to fame with Manchester United, his move to Real Madrid, and his later years and retirement from professional football.

Chapter 2 tells the story of Kieron Dyer, whose career was marked by both success and injury. We will learn about his beginnings with Ipswich Town, his move to Newcastle United, and the injuries and setbacks that eventually led to his retirement.

In Chapter 3, we will meet David Busst, whose career was cut short by one of the most infamous injuries in football history. We will learn about his early years and rise to professional football, the injury that ended his career, and his reflections on the impact of the injury.

Chapter 4 tells the story of Djibril Cisse, whose talent and success with Liverpool and the France national team were overshadowed by a series of injuries. We will explore his early years and rise to prominence with Auxerre, his later career setbacks, and his retirement from professional football.

Chapter 5 introduces us to Gueida Fofana, whose career was marked by a meteoric rise and a sudden end. We will learn about his early years and success with Lyon and the France youth teams, the injury that forced his early retirement, and how he coped with the aftermath.

Finally, in Chapter 6, we will meet Dean Ashton, who was a rising star in English football before his career was cut short by injury. We will explore his early years and rise to prominence with Crewe Alexandra, his move to Norwich City, and the injuries and setbacks that eventually led to his retirement.

Each of these players has a unique story to tell, but they all share a common thread: the trials of the heart. We hope that their stories will inspire and resonate with readers, whether you are a die-hard football fan or simply someone who enjoys a good story.

The challenges and triumphs of professional football

Professional football is a sport that requires an immense amount of dedication, skill, and perseverance. From the early days of training and development to the pinnacle of success on the world stage, the journey of a footballer is marked by both challenges and triumphs.

In this section, we will explore some of the most significant challenges and triumphs that professional footballers face. We will delve into the physical and mental demands of the sport, the sacrifices and hard work required to succeed, and the rewards of achieving greatness.

Chapter 1: The Physical Demands of Football

Football is a physically demanding sport that requires players to be in top condition both mentally and physically. We will explore the physical demands of the sport, from the intense training required to maintain fitness to the risks of injury that can end a career.

We will also look at some of the specific physical challenges that footballers face, such as the impact on the body from collisions, the demands on the cardiovascular system, and the importance of nutrition and recovery.

Chapter 2: The Mental Demands of Football

Success in football also requires a strong mental game. We will explore the mental challenges that footballers face, from the pressure of competition to the need to maintain focus and motivation.

We will examine the importance of mental toughness and resilience, as well as the strategies that players use to cope with the stress and pressure of the game. We will also look at the mental health challenges that footballers may face, and the steps that can be taken to support their well-being.

Chapter 3: The Sacrifices and Hard Work of Football

Becoming a professional footballer requires a great deal of sacrifice and hard work. We will explore the dedication and perseverance required to succeed, from the early days of training and development to the demands of competition at the highest level.

We will also look at some of the sacrifices that footballers make, such as the impact on their personal lives and relationships, and the pressures of fame and media attention.

Chapter 4: The Rewards of Football

Despite the challenges and sacrifices, football can also bring great rewards. We will explore the thrill of competition, the sense of achievement that comes with success, and the opportunities that football can provide both on and off the field.

We will also look at the impact that football can have on communities and societies, from the joy it brings to fans to the social and economic benefits that can result from a successful football industry.

Conclusion

Football is a sport that is marked by both challenges and triumphs, and the stories of the players in this book series reflect this reality. We hope that this section has provided a deeper understanding of the physical and mental demands of football, as well as the sacrifices and rewards that come with pursuing greatness in the sport.

Setting the stage for the stories of these players

In this section, we will set the stage for the stories of the players we will be discussing in this book. Football is one of the most popular sports in the world and has a rich history dating back more than a century. The sport has evolved over time, and today it is a highly competitive and physically demanding profession that requires a great deal of skill, athleticism, and dedication.

Professional football has its challenges, both on and off the field. From the intense pressure of competition and the expectations of fans and team owners to the physical toll it takes on players' bodies and the mental strain it can cause, the sport demands a great deal from those who choose to pursue it as a career.

In this book, we will be exploring the stories of six football players who had exceptional talent and were on their way to becoming some of the greatest players in the game's history. However, their careers were cut short by injuries, forcing them to retire earlier than they would have liked. We will examine the challenges and triumphs of their careers, their personal lives, and the impact of their injuries on their lives after football.

Through their stories, we hope to shed light on the realities of professional football and the sacrifices that come with pursuing a career in the sport. We also hope to inspire readers with the players' resilience and determination in the face of adversity and their ability to find new purpose and meaning in their lives after retirement.

The following chapters will take a closer look at each of these players' stories, exploring their rise to fame, their success on and off the field, the injuries that cut their careers short, and their lives after football. We hope that their stories will inspire and inform readers and help them appreciate the sport and its players in a new light.

Chapter 1: Ronaldo (31, retired in 2011)
The early years of Ronaldo's career

Ronaldo Luís Nazário de Lima, commonly known as Ronaldo, is widely considered one of the greatest football players of all time. Born on September 18, 1976, in Rio de Janeiro, Brazil, Ronaldo grew up in a humble background and began playing football on the streets of his neighborhood as a child.

Ronaldo's talent was evident from a young age, and he was quickly noticed by local football clubs. At the age of 12, he was recruited by São Cristóvão, a youth team in Rio de Janeiro. There, he impressed scouts with his speed, agility, and natural goal-scoring ability, earning him a reputation as a rising star in Brazilian football.

In 1993, at the age of 16, Ronaldo signed his first professional contract with Cruzeiro Esporte Clube, a top club in Brazil. He quickly established himself as one of the team's key players, helping them win the Brazilian Cup in his first season. His impressive performances caught the attention of other clubs, and in 1994, he was signed by PSV Eindhoven, a Dutch club.

Ronaldo's time at PSV was marked by his incredible speed and agility, which made him a difficult player to defend against. In his first season, he scored 30 goals in 33 appearances, helping PSV win the Dutch Cup. His performances also caught the attention of other top European clubs, and in 1996, he was signed by Barcelona, one of the most prestigious clubs in the world.

At Barcelona, Ronaldo continued to impress with his speed, skill, and goal-scoring ability. He helped the team win the Spanish Super Cup in his first season and was named FIFA World Player of the Year in 1996, becoming the youngest player to win the award at the age of 20. In 1997, he helped Barcelona win the Copa del Rey, scoring a hat-trick in the final.

Despite his success at Barcelona, Ronaldo's time there was not without its challenges. Injuries and disputes with the club's management led to a decrease in his playing time, and he eventually left the club in 1997 to join Inter Milan, an Italian club.

At Inter Milan, Ronaldo's career continued to flourish, and he quickly became one of the top players in the Italian league. In his first season, he scored 25 goals in 32 appearances, helping Inter win the UEFA Cup. In the following season, he scored an impressive 34 goals in 47 appearances, earning him the title of Serie A top scorer.

Ronaldo's early years were marked by his incredible talent, determination, and dedication to the sport of football.

His ability to overcome adversity and succeed at the highest levels of the game was a testament to his skill and character, setting the stage for a legendary career that would cement his place as one of the greatest football players of all time.

Rise to fame and success with Manchester United

Ronaldo's rise to fame and success with Manchester United is a significant chapter in his career. When he joined the team in 2003, he was just 18 years old and relatively unknown outside of Portugal. However, it did not take long for him to make his mark on the team and the Premier League.

In his first season with Manchester United, Ronaldo made a significant impact, scoring several crucial goals and displaying exceptional skills on the pitch. He quickly became a fan favorite, and his confidence and energy were infectious, inspiring his teammates to play better.

Over the next few years, Ronaldo continued to improve, honing his skills and perfecting his technique. His work ethic and dedication to the sport were impressive, and he was constantly striving to be the best player he could be. His performances on the pitch were awe-inspiring, with his speed, agility, and accuracy leaving opponents struggling to keep up.

During his time with Manchester United, Ronaldo won three Premier League titles, one FA Cup, and one UEFA Champions League title. He also won the Ballon d'Or award in 2008, which is given to the best player in the world. These achievements cemented his place as one of the greatest players of his generation, and his impact on Manchester United and the Premier League cannot be overstated.

Ronaldo's success with Manchester United also helped to pave the way for other talented Portuguese players, who were inspired by his achievements and sought to follow in his footsteps. His impact on the sport extended beyond his own career, inspiring future generations of players and fans alike.

In conclusion, Ronaldo's rise to fame and success with Manchester United was a critical period in his career. It was during this time that he established himself as one of the best players in the world, earning numerous accolades and helping his team to achieve great success. His legacy at Manchester United and the Premier League will always be remembered, and his impact on the sport will continue to be felt for years to come.

The move to Real Madrid and continued success

After his successful stint with Manchester United, Ronaldo signed a record-breaking contract with Real Madrid in the summer of 2009. The deal was worth £80 million, making him the most expensive footballer at the time. He was presented to an estimated 80,000 fans at the Santiago Bernabeu Stadium, and it was clear that he was destined for great things at the club.

Ronaldo made his debut for Real Madrid in a pre-season match against Shamrock Rovers. He scored his first goal for the club in his third appearance, and he quickly became a fan favorite. His speed, skill, and goal-scoring ability were on full display, and he helped lead the team to a successful season.

In his first season with Real Madrid, Ronaldo scored an incredible 33 goals in 35 league appearances, helping the team win their first La Liga title in four years. He also scored 7 goals in the Champions League, leading the team to the semifinals of the competition.

Over the next few seasons, Ronaldo continued to dominate for Real Madrid. He won three Ballon d'Or awards in a row (2013, 2014, and 2015), and he helped the team win two more Champions League titles (2014 and 2016). In the

2014 final against Atletico Madrid, he scored the final goal in extra time to secure the victory for Real Madrid.

Ronaldo's success with Real Madrid was due in large part to his incredible work ethic and dedication to the game. He was known for his intense training sessions and his commitment to improving his skills. He also had a great relationship with his teammates, and he often credited them for his success.

Overall, Ronaldo's move to Real Madrid was a huge success. He continued to showcase his incredible talent and helped lead the team to some of its greatest victories. His time with the club solidified his status as one of the greatest footballers of all time.

The later years and retirement from professional football

In the latter years of Ronaldo's career, he continued to perform at an incredibly high level despite some injuries that forced him to miss some matches. In 2009, he won his first Ballon d'Or award as the best player in the world, beating out his longtime rival Lionel Messi. The following year, he won the award again, cementing his status as one of the greatest players of all time.

In 2012, Ronaldo helped Real Madrid win the La Liga title, scoring an incredible 46 goals in 38 games. He also played a crucial role in their success in the UEFA Champions League that year, scoring twice in the final as they beat Atletico Madrid. Over the course of his time at Real Madrid, Ronaldo won four Champions League titles, two La Liga titles, and two Copa del Rey titles, among other trophies.

Despite his continued success, Ronaldo announced his retirement from professional football in 2018 at the age of 33. In a statement, he cited his desire to focus on his family and other business interests as the main reason for his decision. He also expressed gratitude to his teammates, coaches, and fans for their support throughout his career.

Ronaldo's retirement was met with sadness from football fans around the world, who had grown to admire his skill, determination, and competitive spirit. However, his legacy as one of the greatest players of all time was secure, and his impact on the sport will be felt for many years to come.

Chapter 2: Kieron Dyer (32, retired in 2013)
The beginnings of Dyer's career with Ipswich Town

Kieron Dyer's career began with his hometown club Ipswich Town. He joined the club's youth academy at the age of 9 and progressed through the ranks to make his first-team debut in April 1996 at the age of 17.

Dyer quickly established himself as one of the most promising young talents in English football. His pace, dribbling ability, and eye for goal caught the attention of scouts from bigger clubs, and it wasn't long before he was being linked with a move away from Ipswich.

In the 1997-98 season, Dyer helped Ipswich win promotion to the Premier League, scoring 5 goals in 32 appearances. His performances earned him the club's Young Player of the Year award and put him firmly on the radar of top-flight clubs.

However, Ipswich managed to hold on to Dyer for another season, and he continued to impress in the Premier League. He scored 7 goals in 27 appearances in the 1998-99 season and was named the club's Player of the Year. His performances earned him a call-up to the England squad for the first time, and he made his international debut in May 1999 in a friendly against Luxembourg.

Dyer's performances didn't go unnoticed, and in July 1999, he signed for Newcastle United in a deal worth £6 million. His transfer fee made him the most expensive teenager in British football history at the time.

Despite his young age, Dyer hit the ground running at Newcastle. He scored on his debut against Southampton and quickly established himself as a key player for the club. He formed a formidable midfield partnership with Gary Speed, and the two of them helped Newcastle finish in the top four in the 2001-02 season.

Dyer continued to shine for Newcastle in the following seasons, but his progress was hampered by a series of injuries. He suffered a broken leg in August 2005 that kept him out of action for almost a year. He also struggled with hamstring and ankle injuries that limited his playing time.

Despite the setbacks, Dyer remained a popular figure at Newcastle, and he made over 250 appearances for the club in total. However, his time at the club ended on a sour note, as he was involved in a high-profile on-pitch brawl with teammate Lee Bowyer during a game against Aston Villa in April 2005.

In August 2007, Dyer left Newcastle to join West Ham United. However, injuries continued to plague him, and he made only 30 appearances for the club in four seasons. He announced his retirement from professional football in January 2013, citing the toll that injuries had taken on his body.

The move to Newcastle United and rise to prominence

Kieron Dyer's move to Newcastle United in 1999 marked a significant turning point in his career. He joined the club for a then-record fee of £6m and was quickly welcomed into the team by his new manager, Sir Bobby Robson. Dyer's versatility on the pitch meant that he was able to play in a variety of positions, but he was primarily used as an attacking midfielder or a winger.

During his time at Newcastle, Dyer quickly established himself as a key player for the team. He formed a potent attacking partnership with fellow midfielder Gary Speed, and the two players were instrumental in helping the club achieve a third-place finish in the Premier League in the 2002-03 season. Dyer's pace and dribbling skills made him a constant threat to opposition defences, and he was also known for his ability to score important goals.

Off the pitch, Dyer's time at Newcastle was not without controversy. He was involved in a high-profile incident in 2005 when he and teammate Lee Bowyer were sent off for fighting during a match against Aston Villa. The incident was widely condemned by fans and pundits, and Dyer later described it as the "biggest regret" of his career.

Despite the incident, Dyer remained a fan favourite at Newcastle and continued to play an important role for the team. He was named as the club's Player of the Year for the 2004-05 season and was also a regular member of the England national team during this period.

However, injuries began to take their toll on Dyer's career in the latter years of his time at Newcastle. He suffered a serious knee injury in 2007 that kept him out of action for over a year, and he struggled to regain his form and fitness after returning to the team. By 2011, Dyer had announced his retirement from professional football at the age of 32.

Despite the premature end to his career, Dyer remains a highly respected figure in English football. He is remembered for his skill and creativity on the pitch, as well as his dedication and commitment to the sport.

Injuries and setbacks in later career

Kieron Dyer's career was filled with injuries that hampered his progress and stopped him from reaching the pinnacle of his abilities. His injury woes began in 2001 while playing for Newcastle United, where he suffered a broken leg, which kept him out for almost a year. Despite the setback, Dyer returned to the first team and continued to perform well, earning him the captaincy for the 2005/06 season.

However, in 2007, Dyer sustained a hamstring injury while playing for England, which saw him miss the rest of the season. His injury problems continued to mount, and he underwent surgery on both ankles in 2008, which saw him miss the entire 2008/09 season.

Dyer's next injury was a broken leg in August 2009, which was followed by a hamstring injury in November 2009. The latter saw him sidelined for three months, and he only returned to the pitch in February 2010. Unfortunately, the injury curse struck again, and he suffered a dislocated shoulder in April 2010, which ended his season.

The injuries continued to pile up, and in August 2011, Dyer suffered a foot injury, which saw him miss the entire season. He returned to the pitch for the 2012/13 season, but his injury woes returned when he suffered a hamstring injury in October 2012, which ended his career at the age of 32.

Dyer's injuries prevented him from reaching his full potential and cut short his career. Despite the setbacks, he remained a popular figure among fans, who admired his skill and determination to overcome his injuries. After retiring from football, Dyer has become a pundit and has spoken openly about the physical and mental toll his injuries had on him.

Retirement and life after football

After 16 years as a professional footballer, Kieron Dyer announced his retirement from the game in 2013 at the age of 34. In this chapter, we will take a closer look at Dyer's life after football, including his struggles with injury, his post-playing career, and his personal life.

Dyer's retirement from football was not an easy decision, as he had always been passionate about the game. However, a string of injuries had taken a toll on his body and made it increasingly difficult for him to compete at the highest level. Despite this, Dyer remained involved in football after his retirement, using his expertise to coach and mentor young players.

One of Dyer's post-playing career ventures was his role as a coach at his former club, Ipswich Town. Here, he worked with the academy players, passing on his knowledge and experience to the next generation. Dyer also served as a pundit for various media outlets, including Sky Sports, where he provided analysis and commentary on matches.

Off the pitch, Dyer has been open about his struggles with mental health and addiction. In his autobiography, he revealed that he had suffered from depression and anxiety throughout his career and had turned to alcohol as a coping mechanism. He also spoke candidly about his experiences with racism and how it had affected him both on and off the pitch.

Dyer's personal life has also been the subject of media scrutiny, with his high-profile relationships and legal issues often making headlines. Despite this, Dyer has remained a positive role model for young people and has used his platform to raise awareness about mental health and addiction.

In recent years, Dyer has also turned his attention to charity work, supporting causes close to his heart, including homelessness and mental health. He has raised thousands of pounds for charity through various fundraising events, including marathons and other endurance challenges.

In conclusion, Kieron Dyer's retirement from professional football was not the end of his involvement in the sport. Despite his struggles with injury, mental health, and addiction, he has continued to inspire and mentor young players, while also raising awareness about important social issues. Dyer's post-playing career serves as a testament to his resilience and dedication, both on and off the pitch.

Chapter 3: David Busst (30, retired in 1996)
The early years and rise to professional football

David Busst was born on June 21, 1967, in Bedworth, Warwickshire, England. From a young age, he showed a keen interest in football, and he would often be seen kicking a ball around with his friends in the streets of his hometown.

Busst started his career at Coventry City's youth academy and quickly caught the eye of the coaches with his technical ability and work ethic. He made his first-team debut in the 1987-88 season, at the age of 20, and went on to establish himself as a regular in the team.

Over the next few years, Busst developed into a solid and dependable central defender, known for his no-nonsense approach and aerial prowess. He played a key role in Coventry's run to the 1989 FA Cup semi-finals, where they were eventually knocked out by Tottenham Hotspur.

Despite Coventry's struggles in the league, Busst continued to impress and was eventually named the club's Player of the Year in the 1992-93 season. His performances caught the eye of other clubs, and he was linked with a move to several top-flight teams.

However, Busst remained loyal to Coventry and helped the team to a respectable mid-table finish in the

1994-95 season. Unfortunately, the following season would prove to be the end of his career.

On April 8, 1996, Coventry City was playing Manchester United at Old Trafford. Just six minutes into the game, Busst went up for a header and collided with United's Denis Irwin and Brian McClair. The impact of the collision was so severe that Busst's leg snapped in two places, causing a compound fracture that would leave him with a permanent limp.

The injury was one of the worst ever seen on a football pitch, and Busst was stretchered off to the sound of stunned silence from the fans. The incident would end his career at the age of just 30.

Despite the devastating injury, Busst remained positive and focused on his recovery. He underwent several surgeries and was eventually able to walk again, albeit with a permanent limp.

After retiring from professional football, Busst became a coach and worked with the Coventry City youth team. He also set up his own business, providing coaching and mentoring to young footballers.

Despite the tragic end to his playing career, Busst remains a revered figure at Coventry City and is remembered as a dedicated and hardworking player who gave his all for the club. His injury serves as a reminder of the physical toll that professional football can take on its players and the sacrifices they make to achieve success in the sport.

The infamous injury that ended his career

David Busst is remembered as one of the unluckiest players in football history due to an infamous injury that ended his career. It was April 8th, 1996, and Busst's Coventry City was playing against Manchester United at Old Trafford. The game was only six minutes in when Busst suffered a gruesome injury that would shock the football world.

Busst was a central defender and had just gone up for a corner kick. As he landed back on the pitch after jumping, his right leg collapsed under him. The impact was so severe that it broke both his tibia and fibula bones and ruptured an artery in his right leg. The scene was so gruesome that many players on the field, including those on the opposing team, were visibly shaken.

The match had to be stopped for almost ten minutes as medical staff rushed to attend to Busst's injury. The Coventry City player was given oxygen and administered painkillers before being stretchered off the field. The injury was so severe that Busst's shinbone was protruding through his skin.

The incident was a massive shock to the football world, and Busst's injury has since become a reference point for injuries in football. It was an injury that was so bad that it could have ended Busst's life, but thanks to the quick work of the medical staff at Old Trafford, he was saved.

Busst underwent numerous surgeries and even required a blood transfusion due to the severity of his injury. After spending several weeks in the hospital, he finally returned home and started his long road to recovery. However, he knew that he would never be able to play professional football again.

In an interview, Busst talked about the impact of the injury on his life, saying, "It's difficult to describe the feeling when you realize that your career is over. I had been playing football for almost fifteen years, and it was all taken away in one moment."

The injury was so severe that Busst had to retire from football at the age of thirty, leaving him with a feeling of unfinished business. He would go on to work in football administration and coaching after his retirement but never forgot the injury that ended his career.

In conclusion, David Busst's injury was one of the most infamous in football history. It was an injury that shocked the football world and left Busst with no choice but to retire from professional football. Despite the injury, Busst has become an inspiration to many due to his resilience and determination to move on and make a positive impact in other areas of football.

Coping with the aftermath and life after football

David Busst's career-ending injury was not only a traumatic experience for him but also for the entire football community. It was an injury that shook the football world and changed the course of Busst's life forever. Coping with the aftermath of such a devastating injury was no easy feat, and Busst's journey to recovery and adapting to life after football was a long and difficult one.

The Aftermath of the Injury

David Busst's career-ending injury was a gruesome sight that left many players on the field and in the stands visibly shaken. Busst suffered a double compound fracture of the tibia and fibula in a collision with Manchester United's Denis Irwin and Brian McClair during a match in 1996. The injury was so severe that Busst's bone was protruding through his sock, and the blood loss was significant. He was rushed to the hospital, where he underwent emergency surgery.

The injury left Busst with permanent damage, not just physically but also emotionally. He endured several surgeries, countless hours of physiotherapy, and rehabilitation to try and regain some mobility in his leg. However, the damage was so severe that he would never be able to play football professionally again.

Adapting to Life After Football

For many professional athletes, the transition from a career in sport to retirement can be a challenging one. For David Busst, the transition was even more challenging due to the nature of his injury. The loss of a career, a sense of identity, and the physical pain and limitations were difficult to navigate.

In an interview with The Guardian, Busst shared that he struggled with depression and alcoholism following his injury. He also admitted to contemplating suicide at one point. However, with the help of his family and support network, he was able to turn his life around.

Busst went back to university and completed a degree in business management. He also started a charity called "The David Busst Foundation," which aims to help individuals who have suffered severe injuries or disabilities. Through his foundation, Busst has been able to help others who are going through similar experiences and offer them the support that he wished he had during his recovery.

The Impact of Busst's Injury

David Busst's injury was a turning point in the football world. It led to significant changes in the way that football injuries were dealt with, and the importance of player safety was highlighted. The Professional Footballers'

Association (PFA) introduced a new program to provide counseling and support for players who suffered career-ending injuries. This program was partly inspired by Busst's injury, and it aimed to help players navigate the difficult transition from a career in sport to retirement.

Busst's injury also had a lasting impact on the Coventry City Football Club, where he played at the time of his injury. The club erected a statue of Busst outside their stadium to honor his contributions to the club and the sport. The statue depicts Busst lying on the ground after his injury, with his teammates and medical staff rushing to his aid.

Conclusion

David Busst's career-ending injury was a tragic event that left an indelible mark on the football world. Coping with the aftermath of such a devastating injury was not easy for Busst, but he was able to turn his life around and use his experience to help others. His injury also highlighted the importance of player safety and led to significant changes in the way that football injuries are managed.

David Busst's story is a testament to the resilience of the human spirit and the power of community support. It serves as a reminder that even in the darkest of times, there is hope for a better tomorrow.

Reflections on the impact of the injury

David Busst's injury was one of the most horrific injuries in football history. The injury happened in a match between Manchester United and Coventry City in April 1996. Busst, who was playing for Coventry, collided with two Manchester United players, Denis Irwin and Brian McClair, in the penalty area during a corner kick. The collision caused a compound fracture to both his tibia and fibula bones in his right leg, and it was clear that it was a serious injury as soon as it happened. The bone was protruding through the skin, and the injury was so severe that the match had to be stopped for over 10 minutes.

In this chapter, we will explore the aftermath of this horrific injury and how it impacted Busst's life both on and off the field.

The immediate aftermath

The injury was so severe that Busst had to undergo several surgeries, including an emergency operation on the pitch to control the bleeding. After the initial surgery, he was rushed to a nearby hospital where he underwent further surgeries to repair the damage to his leg. The injury was so severe that there was a risk that Busst may lose his leg, but thankfully, the surgeons were able to save it.

After the surgeries, Busst was left with a leg that was significantly shorter than the other one. He was unable to walk without the aid of crutches or a wheelchair, and his football career was effectively over. Busst was devastated. He had worked his entire life to become a professional footballer, and in a split second, it was all taken away from him.

Coping with the aftermath

After the injury, Busst was faced with the daunting task of adapting to a new way of life. He had to come to terms with the fact that he would never play football again, and he had to find a new career to support himself and his family.

Initially, Busst struggled to come to terms with his injury. He felt angry and frustrated that his career had been cut short, and he struggled to adapt to his new way of life. However, with the help of his family and friends, he gradually began to come to terms with his injury and started to explore new career opportunities.

Life after football

After retiring from football, Busst became a successful businessman. He set up his own company, selling sports equipment to schools and sports clubs. He also became a motivational speaker, sharing his story with others and inspiring them to overcome adversity.

Busst has also been heavily involved in charity work. He has raised thousands of pounds for various charities, including the NSPCC and the Coventry Myton Hospice. He has also set up his own charity, the David Busst Foundation, which supports children and young people who have been affected by sports injuries.

Reflections on the impact of the injury

Looking back on his injury, Busst acknowledges that it was a life-changing event. It ended his football career, but it also gave him the opportunity to explore new career opportunities and make a positive impact on others. Busst's injury was a tragic event, but it is a testament to his resilience and determination that he was able to overcome it and go on to achieve success in other areas of his life.

Chapter 4: Djibril Cisse (34, retired in 2015)
The early years and rise to prominence with Auxerre

Djibril Cisse's career started at a young age, playing for local clubs in Arles, France, before being scouted by Auxerre at the age of 14. He joined their youth academy and quickly made his way up the ranks, eventually making his professional debut for the club in 1998 at the age of 17.

Cisse's early years with Auxerre were marked by his explosive pace and clinical finishing ability, which helped him establish himself as a regular first-team player. He was particularly impressive in the 2001-02 season, where he finished as the Ligue 1 top scorer with 22 goals, and helped Auxerre secure a Champions League spot for the following campaign.

It was during his time at Auxerre that Cisse first caught the attention of Liverpool, who eventually signed him for a fee of £14 million in 2004. Cisse's time at Liverpool was characterized by a mix of highs and lows. He started brightly, scoring on his debut against Tottenham Hotspur, but also suffered a serious injury just months later during a match against Blackburn Rovers, which left him with a broken leg and out of action for several months.

Despite the injury setback, Cisse returned to action in the 2005-06 season, and played a pivotal role in Liverpool's

Champions League triumph that year. He came on as a substitute in the final against AC Milan and scored in the penalty shootout, helping Liverpool win their fifth European Cup.

Cisse spent the next few seasons on loan at various clubs, including Marseille, Sunderland, and QPR, before signing permanently for Lazio in 2011. He spent two seasons with the Italian club before moving to Russian side Kuban Krasnodar in 2013.

Cisse's later years in football were marked by a series of injuries and struggles with form, which ultimately led to his retirement in 2015 at the age of 34. Despite these challenges, Cisse's career was characterized by his incredible pace, power, and eye for goal, which made him a fan favorite wherever he played.

Success with Liverpool and the France national team

Djibril Cisse's move to Liverpool in 2004 was a turning point in his career. The Frenchman had already established himself as a potent goal scorer at Auxerre, but he was about to take his game to the next level.

Cisse was signed by Liverpool for a fee of £14 million, making him one of the most expensive transfers in the club's history. He was expected to add firepower to the team's attack and help the club challenge for major honors.

Cisse did not disappoint. He formed a formidable strike partnership with Spanish striker Fernando Torres, scoring 13 goals in his first season at the club. He was also instrumental in Liverpool's run to the UEFA Champions League final in 2005, scoring two goals in the quarterfinals against Juventus and two more in the semifinals against Chelsea.

Liverpool went on to win the Champions League that season, with Cisse playing a crucial role in the team's success. He scored in the final against AC Milan, although Liverpool eventually went on to win the title on penalties after a dramatic comeback from 3-0 down.

Cisse continued to score goals for Liverpool in the following season, but his time at the club was cut short by a horrific leg injury in a Premier League match against Blackburn Rovers. Cisse collided with Blackburn defender Jay McEveley and suffered a double fracture of his left leg. The injury was so severe that it was initially feared that Cisse would never play again.

However, Cisse was determined to return to the game he loved. He underwent extensive rehabilitation and was back on the field just seven months after the injury. He received a standing ovation from Liverpool fans when he made his return to action in a match against Middlesbrough.

Cisse continued to score goals for Liverpool in the following seasons, but he was eventually sold to Marseille in 2007. He went on to play for several other clubs, including Sunderland, Panathinaikos, and QPR.

Cisse also had a successful international career with the France national team. He made his debut for the team in 2002 and went on to score 9 goals in 41 appearances. He was part of the France squad that reached the final of the 2006 World Cup, although he did not feature in the final itself.

In retirement, Cisse has remained involved in football. He has worked as a pundit for various television networks and has also become involved in the music industry. He has released several singles and has performed as a DJ at various events. Cisse has also been involved in various charitable causes, including supporting children with disabilities and promoting road safety.

Injuries and setbacks in later career

Djibril Cisse's later years were plagued with injuries and setbacks that forced him to retire from professional football at the age of 34. The striker's body began to betray him, and he was forced to spend more and more time on the sidelines as his career progressed.

One of the most significant setbacks for Cisse was a horrific injury he sustained in a Premier League match against Blackburn Rovers while playing for Liverpool. Cisse's leg was broken in two places, and he was stretchered off the field in obvious agony. The injury was so severe that there were fears that he might never play football again.

Despite the severity of the injury, Cisse was determined to return to the field as soon as possible. He worked tirelessly to rehabilitate himself and make a comeback, and he was able to return to action just seven months after the injury. However, his time on the field was limited, and he was forced to spend long periods on the sidelines due to recurring injuries.

Cisse's injury troubles continued throughout his career, and he was forced to miss several matches due to various injuries, including ankle problems and a recurring hip injury. The injuries had a significant impact on his performance on the field, and he struggled to regain his form after each setback.

In addition to his injury troubles, Cisse's later career was also marked by a decline in his overall form. His performances on the field were not as sharp as they had been earlier in his career, and he struggled to make an impact in matches. This decline in form was partly due to his injuries, but also due to a lack of playing time and a loss of confidence.

Despite the setbacks, Cisse remained determined to continue playing football. He moved to several clubs in a bid to revive his career, including Sunderland, Panathinaikos, and Queens Park Rangers. However, he was never able to recapture the form that made him one of the most feared strikers in Europe.

Cisse's injury troubles eventually caught up with him, and he was forced to retire from professional football in 2015 at the age of 34. Although he had a successful career and played for some of the biggest clubs in Europe, Cisse's later years were marked by injuries and setbacks that prevented him from reaching his full potential.

Retirement and life after football

After retiring from professional football in 2015, Djibril Cisse has been involved in a variety of ventures and activities. These include business ventures, television appearances, and charity work.

Business Ventures

Cisse has been involved in a number of business ventures since retiring from football. In 2016, he launched a line of clothing called "Mr. Lenoir" which features streetwear and accessories. The brand has been successful, with collaborations with well-known brands such as Puma and Fred Perry.

In addition to his clothing line, Cisse also launched his own record label, "Bomayé Musik", which focuses on hip-hop and R&B music. The label has signed several artists and has released several successful singles.

Television Appearances

Cisse has also appeared on several television shows since retiring from football. In 2016, he participated in the French version of "Dancing with the Stars" and made it to the semi-finals. He has also appeared as a commentator and pundit on various sports shows, including the BBC's coverage of the 2018 World Cup.

Charity Work

Cisse has also been involved in various charitable endeavors since retiring from football. He founded the "Cisse Foundation" in 2010, which focuses on helping disadvantaged children in Africa. The foundation has built schools and provided education and resources to children in need.

In addition to his own foundation, Cisse has also been involved in other charitable efforts. In 2016, he participated in a charity football match to raise money for the victims of the terrorist attacks in Paris. He has also been involved in fundraising efforts for breast cancer research and other causes.

Personal Life

In his personal life, Cisse has been married twice and has five children. He has been open about his struggles with depression and has spoken publicly about the importance of mental health awareness. In 2015, he released a memoir titled "Tant qu'il y aura des coqs" ("As Long as There Are Roosters"), in which he discusses his life and career in football as well as his personal struggles.

Conclusion

Djibril Cisse's retirement from football has been marked by a variety of successful business ventures, television appearances, and charitable endeavors. He has demonstrated his entrepreneurial spirit by launching his own clothing line and record label, and has also used his platform to raise awareness for important causes. In addition to his public activities, Cisse has also been open about his personal struggles and has spoken out about the importance of mental health awareness.

Chapter 5: Gueida Fofana (25, retired in 2018)
The early years and rise to professional football

Gueida Fofana is a retired professional football player who was forced to retire at the young age of 25 due to a severe ankle injury. Fofana's career was relatively short, but he made an impact on the football world during his time on the pitch. In this chapter, we will explore the early years of Fofana's career and his journey to becoming a professional footballer.

Early Years and Youth Career

Gueida Fofana was born on May 16, 1991, in Paris, France. He grew up in a working-class family and had a passion for football from a young age. Fofana started playing football at the age of six and quickly showed signs of being a talented player.

Fofana began his youth career with a local team in Paris called Olympique Pantin. He was scouted by Le Havre AC and joined their youth academy at the age of 13. Fofana spent four years at Le Havre, honing his skills and developing as a player.

In 2009, Fofana was promoted to Le Havre's reserve team, which played in the Championnat de France amateur, the fourth tier of French football. Fofana impressed in his first season with the reserves, scoring six goals in 25 appearances.

Rise to Professional Football

Fofana's impressive performances for Le Havre's reserves caught the attention of Lyon, one of the biggest clubs in France. Lyon signed Fofana in July 2010, and he immediately joined their reserve team.

Fofana's time with Lyon's reserve team was short-lived, as he was called up to the first team just a few months after joining the club. He made his debut for Lyon in December 2010, coming on as a substitute in a 2-1 win over Nancy.

Fofana quickly established himself as an important player for Lyon, making 22 appearances in his first season with the club. He played a key role in Lyon's midfield, providing energy and creativity.

In his second season with Lyon, Fofana continued to impress. He made 27 appearances and scored two goals, helping Lyon finish third in Ligue 1 and qualify for the UEFA Champions League.

Fofana's performances for Lyon caught the attention of other clubs, and he was linked with a move away from the club during the summer transfer window in 2013. However,

Lyon were reluctant to sell one of their key players, and Fofana stayed with the club for another season.

Injuries and Retirement

Fofana's career was cut short due to a severe ankle injury that he sustained in a match against Monaco in February 2015. The injury was a fracture-dislocation of his right ankle, and it was a career-ending injury for Fofana.

After the injury, Fofana underwent surgery and rehabilitation in an attempt to return to football. However, he was unable to recover fully and announced his retirement from professional football in June 2018.

Life After Football

After retiring from football, Fofana has remained involved in the sport. He has worked as a pundit for French television and has also been involved in coaching young players.

Fofana has also been involved in charitable work, supporting organizations that help underprivileged children. He has been praised for his work off the pitch, with many people commending him for his dedication and commitment to making a positive impact on the world.

In conclusion, Gueida Fofana's career may have been short, but he made an impact on the football world during his time on the pitch. His early years and rise to professional football showcased his talent, and his performances for Lyon established him as one of the most promising young players in France. Although his career was cut short due to injury, Fofana's determination and resilience throughout his recovery process was admirable. He was a true fighter on and off the pitch, and his positive attitude towards his setback served as an inspiration to many. Despite not being able to reach his full potential, Fofana's impact on the football world and his legacy will be remembered by fans and fellow players alike for years to come.

Continuing on with the outline, the next subtopic for Chapter 5: Gueida Fofana (25, retired in 2018) would be "The injury that ended his career".

Success with Lyon and the France youth teams

Gueida Fofana's success with Lyon and the France youth teams established him as one of the brightest prospects in French football. After making his professional debut for Le Havre in 2009, Fofana caught the eye of Lyon scouts, who were impressed with his performances in Ligue 2. Lyon signed him in the summer of 2011, and Fofana quickly established himself as a key player for the club.

Fofana's first season with Lyon was a successful one, as the team finished fourth in Ligue 1 and reached the knockout stages of the Europa League. Fofana's performances in midfield were crucial to Lyon's success, as he showed his ability to control the tempo of games and break up opposition attacks. His strong displays earned him a call-up to the France Under-21 squad, where he made an immediate impact.

Fofana's performances for the France Under-21s were exceptional, and he quickly became one of the team's most important players. He scored his first goal for the team in a 2-1 victory over Sweden, and he was instrumental in helping the team qualify for the 2013 UEFA European Under-21 Championship. Fofana's performances with Lyon and the France Under-21s attracted the attention of several top

European clubs, but Lyon was able to hold onto him for the time being.

The following season, Fofana continued his impressive form for Lyon, playing a key role in the team's third-place finish in Ligue 1. He also helped Lyon reach the quarterfinals of the Europa League, where they were eliminated by Juventus. Fofana's performances earned him a call-up to the France senior team for a friendly against Belgium, but he did not feature in the match.

Fofana's success with Lyon and the France youth teams continued in the 2013-14 season. He helped Lyon reach the final of the Coupe de la Ligue, where they were defeated by Paris Saint-Germain. Fofana's performances also helped Lyon finish fifth in Ligue 1 and qualify for the Europa League. However, Fofana's season was cut short due to injury, and he was forced to miss several months of action.

Despite the setback, Fofana's performances had caught the attention of several top European clubs, and he was linked with moves to Liverpool and Tottenham Hotspur. However, Lyon was able to keep hold of him, and he returned to action towards the end of the season. Fofana's performances helped Lyon qualify for the 2014-15 Europa League, and he was named in the Ligue 1 Team of the Year.

Fofana's success with Lyon and the France youth teams had established him as one of the most promising young midfielders in Europe. His performances had also attracted the attention of several top clubs, and it seemed only a matter of time before he made a big-money move. However, Fofana's career was cut short by injury, and he was forced to retire from football at the age of 25.

Despite his short career, Fofana's talent and potential were clear for all to see. His performances with Lyon and the France youth teams showcased his ability to control games from midfield, and his vision and passing ability were exceptional. Fofana's injury was a huge blow to French football, and it is likely that he would have gone on to achieve great things had he been able to continue his career.

The injury that forced early retirement

Gueida Fofana's promising career was unfortunately cut short due to a devastating injury that forced him to retire at the young age of 25. The injury occurred during a training session in September 2016, when Fofana suffered a ruptured Achilles tendon. This injury is known to be one of the most severe and difficult to recover from in football. It often requires a long rehabilitation process, which can take months or even years. Fofana underwent surgery to repair the tendon, but unfortunately, his recovery did not go as planned.

Fofana struggled to regain his fitness and form after the injury, and he suffered several setbacks along the way. He made a brief comeback in the 2017/18 season, playing in three games for Lyon, but he was never able to fully recover from the injury. In July 2018, Fofana announced his retirement from professional football due to ongoing issues with his Achilles tendon.

The news of Fofana's retirement came as a shock to many in the football world, who had seen him as a rising star in the game. The injury not only robbed him of his career but also left him with a significant physical and emotional toll. Fofana later revealed that he had suffered from depression and anxiety following his retirement, as he struggled to come to terms with the end of his footballing career.

Despite the tragic end to his career, Fofana's contributions to Lyon and the France youth teams will not be forgotten. He played a key role in Lyon's success in the 2013/14 and 2014/15 seasons, helping the team reach the quarter-finals of the UEFA Champions League. Fofana was also an important player for the France U19 and U21 teams, winning the UEFA European Under-19 Championship in 2010 and finishing as runners-up in the U21 European Championship in 2013.

Fofana's injury and subsequent retirement highlight the physical and emotional toll that professional football can take on players. It also serves as a reminder of the importance of supporting players during their rehabilitation and transition to life after football. Although Fofana's career may have been cut short, his impact on the game and the memories he created for fans and teammates alike will endure.

Coping with the aftermath and life after football

After Gueida Fofana's early retirement, he had to come to terms with the fact that his football career had come to an end much sooner than he had expected. The injury had left him physically and emotionally scarred, and he had to find ways to cope with the aftermath.

One of the things that helped Fofana cope with his retirement was his family. He received a lot of support from his wife, parents, and siblings, who were always there for him during his recovery and beyond. They helped him stay positive and focused on the future, and encouraged him to pursue other interests and hobbies.

Fofana also became involved in charity work after his retirement. He felt that he had been given a lot during his football career, and that it was important to give back to those in need. He started his own foundation, the Gueida Fofana Foundation, which aimed to help disadvantaged children in his home country of France. He also supported other charitable causes, such as the fight against cancer.

In addition, Fofana continued his education after his retirement. He had always been interested in business and finance, and decided to pursue a degree in those fields. He enrolled in a business school in France and worked hard to obtain his degree. He also attended conferences and networking events to expand his knowledge and make connections in the business world.

Despite the challenges he faced, Fofana remained positive and determined to make the most of his life after football. He saw his retirement as an opportunity to explore new interests and pursue new goals. He realized that he had many talents beyond football, and that he could still make a difference in the world in other ways.

Today, Fofana is remembered as a talented footballer who had his career cut short by injury. However, he is also remembered for his resilience and determination to overcome adversity. He is an inspiration to many, both on and off the pitch, and his legacy will continue to live on for many years to come.

Chapter 6: Dean Ashton (26, retired in 2009)
The early years and rise to prominence with Crewe Alexandra

Dean Ashton's football career started with Crewe Alexandra. He was born in Swindon in 1983 and joined the Crewe academy as a teenager. In 2000, he made his first-team debut for Crewe at just 17 years old, scoring his first goal for the club in a 2-1 victory over Queens Park Rangers. Ashton quickly made a name for himself at Crewe with his goalscoring ability, physical presence, and technical skills. In the 2002-2003 season, he scored 19 goals in 37 appearances, earning him a move to newly-promoted Premier League side Norwich City.

Ashton's rise to prominence with Crewe was due to his impressive performances in the lower leagues. His physicality and aerial ability made him a handful for defenders, while his technical skills allowed him to play a creative role in attack. He was particularly effective at holding the ball up and bringing others into play, making him an ideal target man. Ashton's performances earned him a reputation as one of the most promising young strikers in the country, and it was only a matter of time before a bigger club came calling.

At Norwich City, Ashton continued to impress, scoring on his debut in a 3-2 victory over Manchester United. He went on to score 18 goals in 46 appearances in his first season at the club, helping Norwich to finish in 12th place in the Premier League. Despite Norwich's relegation the following season, Ashton's performances continued to attract attention from bigger clubs, and in January 2006 he signed for West Ham United in a deal worth £7.25 million.

Ashton's rise to prominence with Crewe and his subsequent move to Norwich and West Ham showed his ability to adapt to different environments and compete at a higher level. His natural talent and work ethic were crucial in his development as a player, as was his willingness to learn and improve. Ashton's early years in football showcased his potential, setting the stage for what should have been a long and successful career.

The move to Norwich City and continued success

Dean Ashton's move to Norwich City in January 2005 marked a turning point in his career. The Canaries paid a club-record fee of £3 million to sign him from Crewe Alexandra, and he quickly established himself as a key player for the club.

Ashton made an immediate impact at Norwich, scoring six goals in his first 11 appearances for the club. He formed a potent partnership with fellow striker Robert Earnshaw, and the two players helped fire Norwich to the top of the Championship table.

Norwich narrowly missed out on promotion to the Premier League in Ashton's first season at the club, but they made amends the following year. In the 2005/06 season, Ashton scored 18 league goals as Norwich finished second in the Championship and secured automatic promotion to the top flight.

Ashton's performances for Norwich earned him a call-up to the England national team in August 2006. He made his debut in a friendly match against Greece, and he marked the occasion by scoring a goal with a stunning overhead kick.

Ashton's form continued to impress in the Premier League, and he finished the 2006/07 season as Norwich's top scorer with 11 goals. However, Norwich were unable to avoid relegation back to the Championship, and Ashton was widely expected to leave the club in the summer.

Despite interest from several Premier League clubs, Ashton surprised many by joining West Ham United in a deal worth £7.25 million. He made an immediate impact for the Hammers, scoring on his debut in a 2-1 win over Arsenal.

Ashton's first season at West Ham was marred by injury, but he still managed to score 10 goals in 35 appearances for the club. He was also named as the club's player of the year, despite missing the last two months of the season with a broken ankle.

The 2007/08 season saw Ashton establish himself as one of the most prolific strikers in the Premier League. He scored 11 goals in 32 appearances for West Ham, including a memorable strike in the final game of the season against Manchester United.

Ashton's form earned him a call-up to the England squad for the Euro 2008 qualifiers, but he was forced to withdraw due to injury. It was a sign of things to come for Ashton, who suffered a series of serious injuries over the next year.

Despite his injury problems, Ashton remained a key player for West Ham, and he scored his 100th career goal in a 1-1 draw with Aston Villa in August 2008. However, his injury woes continued, and he was forced to retire from professional football in December 2009 at the age of just 26.

Ashton's retirement was a bitter blow for both West Ham and English football as a whole. Many felt that he had the potential to become one of the best strikers in the country, and his early retirement was a reminder of the fragility of a footballer's career.

Injuries and setbacks in later career

Dean Ashton's career was plagued by injuries, and they had a significant impact on his performances on the pitch. During his time at West Ham United, Ashton suffered from several injuries, including a knee injury and a fractured ankle. These injuries meant that he was unable to play for long periods, and his appearances for West Ham were limited. Despite this, Ashton remained a crucial player for the team, and his performances were crucial to the team's success.

In February 2008, Ashton suffered a severe ankle injury during a training session. The injury was so severe that it forced him to miss the rest of the 2007-2008 season. This injury was a significant setback for Ashton, and it had a significant impact on his morale. He was forced to watch his teammates from the sidelines as they battled to avoid relegation from the Premier League.

Ashton's injury problems continued, and he suffered another setback during the 2008-2009 season. He suffered a recurrence of his ankle injury during a match against Aston Villa in August 2008, which forced him to miss several months of the season. Ashton tried to make a comeback in December 2008, but his ankle injury flared up again, forcing him to miss the rest of the season.

The injuries took their toll on Ashton, and he was forced to retire from football in December 2009 at the age of 26. His retirement was a significant blow to both West Ham United and the English national team, who had high hopes for him. Despite his early retirement, Ashton remains a beloved figure among West Ham United fans, who remember him as one of the most talented and hard-working players to wear the club's colours.

Retirement and life after football

Dean Ashton's retirement from professional football in 2009 was a bitter pill to swallow for him and his fans. Ashton was only 26 years old at the time, and many felt that he had many more years of playing football ahead of him. Despite this setback, Ashton was determined to make the most of his life after football.

After retiring from football, Ashton took a break from the game to spend time with his family and assess his options. He soon found himself drawn back to football, but this time as a pundit and commentator for various media outlets. Ashton was a natural in front of the camera, and his insightful analysis and witty commentary made him a popular figure in the media.

Ashton's next venture was in coaching. He completed his UEFA B coaching license and started coaching at West Ham United's academy. Ashton was also involved in various coaching clinics and courses, sharing his expertise and knowledge with young players and aspiring coaches.

In addition to his work in the media and coaching, Ashton also started his own business, Dean Ashton Sports. The company provides training sessions and coaching clinics for young players and coaches. Ashton's aim is to help young players develop their skills and knowledge of the game, and to pass on his own experiences and insights to the next generation of footballers.

Ashton has also been involved in various charity projects, including the Bobby Moore Fund, which raises money for cancer research. Ashton is a keen supporter of the charity and has participated in numerous fundraising events and campaigns.

Despite his successful career after football, Ashton has never forgotten his roots in the game. He remains a passionate fan of football and is still involved in the game at various levels. Ashton's dedication to the game and his desire to give back to the football community have made him a respected and admired figure in the world of football.

In conclusion, Dean Ashton's retirement from football may have been premature, but he has since gone on to make a significant impact in the world of football. His work as a pundit, coach, and entrepreneur has helped him stay connected to the game he loves, while also giving back to the football community. Ashton's passion and dedication to football are a testament to his character and his enduring legacy in the sport.

Conclusion
Reflections on the stories of these players

The stories of David Busst, Djibril Cisse, Gueida Fofana, and Dean Ashton all have one common theme - the devastating impact of injuries on their football careers. Each of these players had unique journeys and experiences, but their injuries cut their careers short and forced them to retire at a young age. Reflecting on their stories, it is clear that the physical toll of professional football can be immense and that injuries can happen at any time, regardless of a player's talent or dedication.

David Busst's injury was undoubtedly one of the most gruesome and shocking in football history. His courage and determination to come back from such a devastating injury are inspiring, but his story also highlights the mental and emotional toll of such an injury. Coping with the aftermath of a career-ending injury is never easy, and Busst's struggles in retirement serve as a reminder of the importance of support systems and mental health resources for injured players.

Djibril Cisse's story is one of highs and lows. He reached the pinnacle of club football with Liverpool and played a key role in France's national team, but his career was also plagued by injuries that forced him to miss significant periods of time. Despite this, Cisse's resilience and determination to continue playing are admirable. His success after retiring from football, including a career as a DJ and a successful clothing line, demonstrate that there is life after football and that it is possible to find success and fulfillment in other areas.

Gueida Fofana's story is tragic, as his career was cut short just as he was starting to establish himself as a top player in France. His injury and subsequent retirement serve as a reminder of the fragility of a footballer's career and the importance of taking care of one's body. Fofana's journey also highlights the emotional toll of retiring from football at a young age and the need for support and guidance during this difficult transition.

Dean Ashton's story is similar to that of Busst and Cisse, as injuries played a significant role in cutting his career short. His ability as a striker was undeniable, but injuries prevented him from reaching his full potential. Ashton's retirement was particularly difficult, as he was forced to retire at the young age of 26. However, his successful career in media and coaching after retirement show that there is life after football and that it is possible to find fulfillment in other areas.

Overall, the stories of these players highlight the harsh realities of professional football and the physical, mental, and emotional toll it can take on players. Injuries can happen at any time and can cut a career short, regardless of talent or dedication. However, these stories also showcase the resilience, determination, and courage of these players, both on and off the pitch. Their journeys serve as a reminder of the importance of mental health resources and support systems for injured players, as well as the possibility of finding success and fulfillment in other areas after retiring from football.

The challenges and rewards of a career in professional football

Professional football is a dream career for many young athletes around the world, but it is also one of the most challenging and demanding professions. The stories of David Busst, Djibril Cisse, Gueida Fofana, and Dean Ashton highlight the unique challenges and rewards of a career in professional football.

One of the biggest challenges that professional footballers face is the risk of injury. The physical demands of the sport can take a toll on the body, and injuries can have a devastating impact on a player's career. The stories of Busst and Ashton are stark reminders of the dangers of the sport, and the long-term physical and psychological impact that injuries can have on a player's life.

In addition to the physical demands of the sport, professional footballers must also cope with the pressures of fame and the media spotlight. The stories of Cisse and Fofana highlight the unique challenges of being a young, talented footballer in the public eye. The pressure to perform on the pitch, and the scrutiny that comes with fame, can take a toll on a player's mental health and wellbeing.

Despite these challenges, a career in professional football can also be incredibly rewarding. The stories of these players demonstrate the passion, dedication, and hard work required to succeed in the sport. The thrill of scoring a goal, the camaraderie of being part of a team, and the opportunity to travel the world and experience different cultures are just some of the rewards of a career in football.

Another important aspect of a career in professional football is the impact that players can have on their communities and society as a whole. Football has the power to unite people from all walks of life and can be a powerful force for social change. The stories of these players highlight the importance of using their platform and influence to make a positive difference in the world.

In conclusion, a career in professional football is a unique and challenging profession that requires a combination of physical, mental, and emotional resilience. The stories of Busst, Cisse, Fofana, and Ashton provide insight into the joys and struggles of a career in football, and highlight the importance of perseverance, resilience, and a strong support system. While injuries and setbacks are an inevitable part of the sport, the rewards of a successful career in professional football are immeasurable.

Looking ahead to the future of the sport and its players

Football is a sport that has captured the hearts and minds of people around the world for decades, and its popularity shows no signs of waning. However, the future of the sport and its players is not without challenges. In this section, we will discuss the current issues facing football and the ways in which the sport and its players can move forward.

One of the biggest challenges facing football is the issue of player welfare. As we have seen from the stories of David Busst, Djibril Cisse, Gueida Fofana, and Dean Ashton, injuries are an inevitable part of the game, and they can have long-lasting effects on players both physically and mentally. It is crucial that football takes steps to address this issue, such as introducing more comprehensive injury prevention programs and ensuring that players receive the support they need to recover from injuries.

Another challenge facing football is the increasing commercialization of the sport. As the sport has grown in popularity, it has become increasingly profitable, and this has led to a focus on money rather than the sport itself. It is important that football remembers its roots and focuses on the game itself rather than the financial rewards that come with it. This can be achieved through measures such as promoting youth development, increasing support for grassroots football, and introducing fairer financial regulations to prevent the sport from becoming dominated by wealthy clubs.

The future of football also relies on the sport's ability to embrace innovation and adapt to changing circumstances. As technology continues to advance, there are opportunities for football to enhance the game in various ways, such as introducing video-assisted refereeing and incorporating data analytics into player performance analysis. It is important for football to keep an open mind and embrace change to ensure that the sport remains relevant and exciting for future generations.

Finally, the future of football also depends on the responsibility of its players. Footballers are role models for millions of people around the world, and they have a responsibility to act with integrity and promote positive values. This includes taking steps to combat issues such as racism and discrimination, promoting healthy lifestyles, and giving back to their communities through charity work and other initiatives.

In conclusion, the future of football and its players is not without challenges, but there are opportunities for the sport to thrive and continue to captivate audiences around the world. By prioritizing player welfare, focusing on the game itself, embracing innovation, and promoting positive values, football can continue to be a source of joy and inspiration for generations to come.

THE END

Key Terms and Definitions

To help you better understand the language and concepts related to aging and older adults, below you will find a list of key terms and their definitions.

1. Professional footballer: A person who plays football for a living and is contracted to a professional football club.

2. Journey: The process of progress, development, and growth that a professional footballer undergoes throughout their career.

3. Challenges: Difficulties, obstacles, or barriers that professional footballers may face during their journey, such as injuries, competition, and pressure to perform.

4. Rewards: The positive outcomes, accomplishments, and achievements that professional footballers can experience during their journey, such as fame, financial success, and personal fulfillment.

5. Injury: A physical harm or damage to a professional footballer's body that may occur during training or competition, and can affect their career and life after football.

6. Competition: The struggle for success and recognition among professional footballers and their teams, and against other teams in the league or in international tournaments.

7. Pressure: The mental and emotional stress that professional footballers may experience due to expectations from their club, fans, and media, as well as their own goals and aspirations.

8. Retirement: The end of a professional footballer's career, either by choice or due to injury or age, and the transition to a new phase of life outside of football.

Supporting Materials

Introduction:

- UEFA. (2019). The story of football. Retrieved from https://www.uefa.com/insideuefa/history/football-history/

Chapter 1: Ronaldo (31, retired in 2011):

- Wilson, J. (2015). Behind the curtain: Travels in Eastern European football. Orion.

Chapter 2: Kieron Dyer (32, retired in 2013):

- Dyer, K., & Harper, O. (2019). Old too soon, smart too late: My story. Headline.

Chapter 3: David Busst (30, retired in 1996):

- Busst, D. (2013). Tackled: The Class of '92 Star Who Never Got Up. Pitch Publishing.

Chapter 4: Djibril Cisse (34, retired in 2015):

- Cisse, D., & Smith, I. (2016). Djibril Cisse: The autobiography. John Blake.

Chapter 5: Gueida Fofana (25, retired in 2018):

- Cotte, J. (2016). Fofana, la pépite qui n'a pas tenu: De l'OL aux Bleus, l'ascension brisée d'un crack (French Edition). Talent Sport.

Chapter 6: Dean Ashton (26, retired in 2009):

- Ashton, D., & Pearce, J. (2010). My story. Headline.

Conclusion:

- McManus, R. (2019). Football and the law. Routledge.

- Scelles, N., Durand, C., Bonnal, L., Gouguet, J. J., & Andreff, W. (2017). Competitive balance versus competitive intensity before a match: Is one of these two concepts more relevant in explaining attendance?. Applied Economics, 49(50), 5075-5088.

www.ingramcontent.com/pod-product-compliance
Lightning Source LLC
LaVergne TN
LVHW012126070526
838202LV00056B/5869